Selfies:
Picture perfect

By Dr. Jeri Fink

with Donna Paltrowitz

Edited by Donna Paltrowitz, BS, MS, Certified Reading and Education Specialist, Author

Selfies: Picture Perfect

By Dr. Jeri Fink

Published by Book Web Publishing, LTD
Book Web Minis
All rights reserved
Copyright 2018
Original and modified cover art by NaCDS and
CoverDesignStudio.com

To Ricky, my husband, friend, and lifelong partner

and our future,

John, Nicky, Mason, and Emma

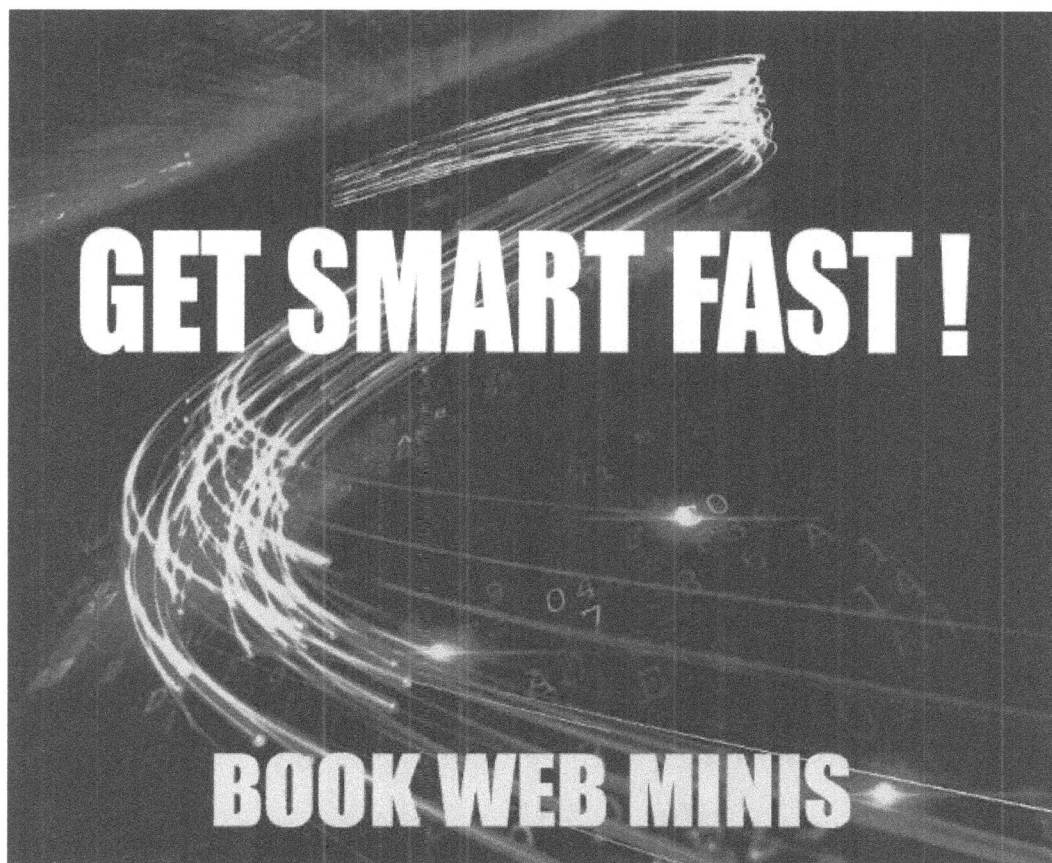

Check out Book Web Fiction at

www.hauntedfamilytrees.com
Amazon #1 Bestsellers in print or ebook

Page turners bursting with haunted family trees, strange lovers, chilling photo insights, and twisted psychopaths burst into life. *Broken Books* reinvent the thriller – blending fact, fiction, and photos into riveting stories you'll never forget. Go to amazon.com to purchase these bestsellers in eBook, print (black & white), and collector's edition (full color print).

Contemporary thrillers:

Broken By Truth (Book 1)

Broken By Birth (Book 2)

Broken By Evil (Book 3)

Don't miss Book Web Historical Fiction

Go back in time to discover how good and evil thrived in the past. Meet the ancestors of the characters in the first three *Broken Books* and follow their legacy.

Broken By Madness (Book 4, Dutch New Amsterdam, 1654)

Broken By Men (Book 5, Spain and Portugal, 1490s)

Broken By Kings (Book 6, Sao Tome, Africa, 1494)

Broken: The Prequel (Book 7, Spanish Inquisition, 15th century)

www.hauntedfamilytrees.com

Love photo insights?

Go to: http:// hauntedfamilytrees.com/ landing-page to get a FREE image each week in your email that will enlighten, inspire, and make you feel good.

The only requirement is a smile.

Selfies: Picture Perfect

Why Selfies? Meet Dr. Jeri Fink

Take control of your selfies!

Everyone snaps selfies! Too often people innocently send the wrong messages.

Professional photographers know exactly how to say what they want. It's all in the details: faces, body language, and background. Learn their secrets and selfie like a pro!

Explore picture play, selfie psychology, and what makes a good selfie. Learn fascinating facts, memes, and stars. Send the messages you want.

Go Picture Perfect!

Dr. Jeri Fink is a bestselling author, photographer, family therapist and clinical social worker. She has written over 30 nonfiction and fiction books for adults and children. Her articles and blogs appear on and offline, including hundreds of topics ranging from psychology, technology, and fiction to humor and family. In *Book Web Minis Series* she explores cutting-edge nonfiction that affirms the power of positive meaning in life.

Donna Paltrowitz began her career as a NYC teacher and licensed reading specialist. Her path evolved into developing, editing, and authoring more than 100 published children's books, adult books, computer books, magazine articles, and educational software. In *Book Web Minis Series*, she explores new paths to affirm positive energy, giving a voice to new discoveries, expert insights, and innovators.

Why Book Web Publishing?

Book Web Publishing produces original mini books in e-book and print formats on positive topics that affect daily living. If you're interested in doing a mini book check out our website, **www.bookwebminis.com** and contact us.

Selfies: Picture Perfect

What does your selfie really say about you?

Contents

1 Wired for Selfies

Selfies freeze the moment – not the whole picture.

It's a photo – snapshot – taken by you and of you, usually on a mobile device and shared with the virtual world. Some are silly, fuzzy, or impulsive. Others are artistic, insightful, or provocative.

Selfies give you the power to change how you appear. You can use facial expressions, emotions, backgrounds, hairstyles, props . . . anything you want. You can enhance, manipulate, and redefine the person inside you. You can tell the world *who* you are, who you want to be, and perhaps most importantly, how you want the world to view *you*.

Selfies get you "seen" in our vast virtual swamp. They empower you to participate, make statements about yourself, connect with others, and get attention. The world is your audience; time, space, and location are not important.

Most of us spend a lot of time in the virtual world. Social media is out of control. Facebook claims over 1.23 billion monthly users; LinkedIn has a modest 347 million users in 200 different countries.

Internet World Stats reports that there are a total of 3,035,749,340 internet users, or 42.3% of the *entire* world population. And growing.

Dr. R. Swaminathan, a Senior Fellow from the *National Internet Exchange of India,* refers to selfies as a "virtual body and digital identity." Selfies are the result of online culture; they have their own logic and process. Simply put, mobile devices produce and deliver a "product" of *you* that is consumed online. Selfies are created, posted, and distributed by the same person. Time, space (public and private) changes, defining a different sense of who you are.

It's no accident they're called selfies.

They're Mini-Me's – self-selected and designed avatars that we use online to give others a sense of who we are.

In 1993, Peter Steiner published a cartoon in *The New Yorker.* It was a drawing of a dog sitting on a chair in front of a computer speaking to a second dog on the floor. The caption read, "On the internet, nobody knows you're a dog." Until 2011, it was the most reproduced cartoon of the magazine.

Only twenty-two years later (2015), Kaamran Hafeez published a cartoon in *The New Yorker,* "Remember when, on the Internet, nobody knew who you were?"

Selfies have changed our visual messages. Is it art or narcissism - a fad or self-expression? Perhaps selfies are all of the above and *more* . . . something that catches our imagination like a virtual wildfire. Yet Selfies weren't born today, they actually have a long history.

2 The first selfie

The first selfie was taken in 1839! That was almost 200 years ago, long before the cell phone was invented. Robert Cornelius was an amateur chemist and photographer from Philadelphia. He set up his camera in the back of the family store and ran into the frame. Remotes didn't exist.

On the back of the image Cornelius wrote "The first light Picture ever taken."

He used a process called "daguerreotype" – an old-looking, often muddy technology of the past.

For twenty years, daguerreotype was the most common form of photography. Making a daguerreotype was long and complicated. A sheet of silver-plated copper had to be polished, treated with mercury vapor fumes, and exposed in a camera from a few seconds to several minutes.

The quality of most Daguerreotype portraits were better than Cornelius' selfie where he had to race the camera. They took time and patience. Below is an 1845 daguerreotype portrait of a photographer.

There were many inventions and years between Cornelius' selfie, large, awkward cameras, daguerreotypes, and your smartphone. Selfies today only need an affordable hand-held device, digital photography instead of film, and "snapshots" without formal sittings. Social media provides s very large audience.

Where did the word selfie come from?

The earliest known use of the word selfie was in a 2002 post from an Australian university student who called himself "Hopey." No one knows his real identity. He took the photo while drunk at a 21st birthday party.

The word caught on.

Eleven years later, in 2013, the Oxford Dictionaries made "selfie" the *WORD OF THE YEAR*. "If it is good enough for the Obamas or The Pope," they explained, "then it is good enough for [us]." The choice was unanimous, partly due to the word's dramatic rise in usage.

Use of the word selfie increased more than 17,000% between October 2012 and 2013 (Oxford Dictionaries).

3 Time Stamps

The idea of selfies or self-portraits has been around as long as humans could create images. In the Middle Ages, monks drew small pictures of themselves in the long texts they copied by hand. Renaissance artists painted self-portraits in oil. Early photographers used mirrors and reflections to capture their images.

The need to see ourselves and how we appear to the world is wired into our brains. You can find it throughout human history. Cavemen created prehistoric art on rock walls, telling stories and showing images of themselves and their worlds.

It carried into Ancient Greece with busts, statues, and funeral reliefs. Rome followed, refining details. By the Early Renaissance, Europeans often put images of themselves in their paintings.

Michelangelo used his face in *The Last Judgement* fresco on the Sistine Chapel and Raphael included himself in his painting, *The School of Athens.*

Albrecht Durer was one of the first artists to paint a series of self-portraits in the 16th century. He was followed by some of the greatest artists of the time: Jan van Eyck, Leonardo DaVinci, Jan Vermeer, Paul Gauguin, and Rembrandt. Rembrandt painted the most self-portraits – 100 during his lifetime. Below is his etching called *Rembrandt with cap pulled forward.*

#LC-USZ72-18

In 1889, one of the most famous artists in the world, post-impressionist Vincent Van Gogh, painted this self-portrait.

Art, like technology, evolves. The painting below, a 1906 self-portrait by Paula Modersohn-Becker is a perfect example of how artists change, seeing the same things but using new ideas, styles, and techniques to reflect the times.

Creative Commons

Today we don't have to be artists or sculptors to create self-portraits. All we need are cellphones, tablets, cameras, or other mobile digital devices.

What's the difference between a Van Gogh and your selfie?

A self-portrait takes time, planning, thought, and skill. A selfie is spontaneous, easy, and you don't have to be Rembrandt or Van Gogh. A self-portrait is expected to last – a statement in time and art. A selfie is about today and spreading your image everywhere on social media.

Self-portraits and selfies are both time stamps.

Who are we? What do we look like? See us – we're here.

4 Vintage Selfies: The Photo Booth

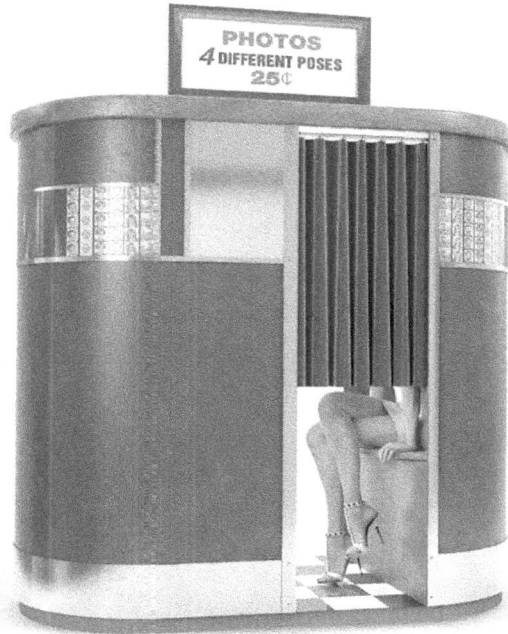

In 1925, Serbian photographer, Anatol Josepho, dramatically changed how people saw themselves. He created a selfie available in the *Photomaton* – a curtain-enclosed booth where people could take pictures of themselves. It cost 25 cents and produced 4 shots in 8 minutes. Within 20 years there were more than 30,000 Photomatons in the U.S. Josepho became a millionaire.

Photomatons became Photo Booths in the 1950s and 60s, utilizing new technology, business deals, and public demand. They were everywhere from drug stores to strip malls. They produced fun black and white strips of photos. Later in the 1970s, color was added.

Eventually, the chemical-based photo machines were replaced by digitals – faster and better quality.

Who needs a photobooth when you can take selfies with your smartphone?

Photo Booth popularity declined until they were used mostly for IDs like passports and driving licenses. Yet they're still around.

Today's photobooths are fully customized selfie stations with names like Mirror Me and MirMir. They're rented for corporate affairs, weddings, Bar Mitzvahs, and other parties. They usually have no walls and come with customized signs and props. Some can text, email, and share on social media. Others offer voice recordings, movement, and animation. Photo Booths, in one form or another, will be around for a long time!

5 Simply Selfie

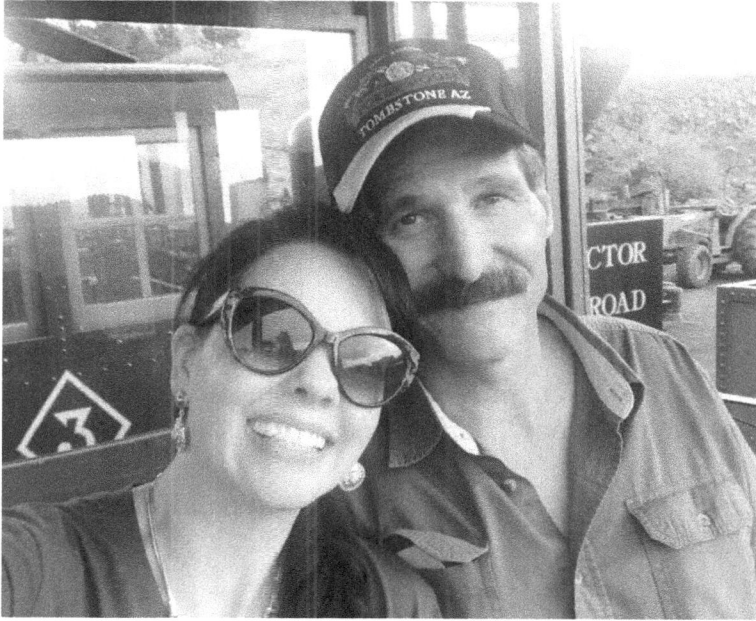

Selfies have come a long way. It's hard to go a day without seeing, receiving, or taking a selfie. There's even a famous monkey selfie when a black macaque (monkey) in an Indonesian jungle, snapped a selfie using a wildlife photographer's camera. There was a big legal battle over who owned the rights. Can an animal own a copyright? It was decided that David Slater, the photographer, owned the copyright. The monkey had no comment.

All of which tells us how much selfies are a part of our lives. Whether human or otherwise, playful or offensive, selfies have basic elements that make them different from other photos. Check out the following details:

*Selfies are casual, informal, and spontaneous.

*The photographer is the subject (or one of them) whether it's a direct image, reflection, or in a mirror.

*A selfie can be an individual shot, couple shot, or group shot.

*Images are usually taken at arm's length (or selfie-stick length), often distorting faces, hands, and other "props." Sometimes a selfie is taken with a remote.

*Selfies are taken by everyone from celebrities and politicians to regular men, women, and kids.

*A selfie tells a story.

*A selfie reveals a moment in time.

*Selfies show up online in social media such as Facebook, Twitter, Instagram, Snapchat.

*A selfie can define you – be careful.

*There are trends in selfies like groupies, foot selfies, shameless selfies, naked selfies, gym selfies, sex selfies, travel selfies . . . anything goes.

*Every day new accessories are developed to improve selfies.

Likes, followers, and friends.

The more you have . . . the better.

Shakira has over 86 *million* likes on her Facebook page.

Katy Perry was the first to reach 100 *million* followers on Twitter.

Rihanna has more than 60 *million* friends on Facebook.

The more the merrier. Why? Whether you're Rihanna or Jane/John Doe, likes, followers, and friends mean *approval*. If that approval is for your selfie, it's proof that you're really great! Selfies put people in control of their image – how they appear to the world – rating in likes, followers, and friends. Accuracy is secondary.

6 What's Your Type?

There are hundreds of selfie types with more created every day. Below are a few of the most popular:

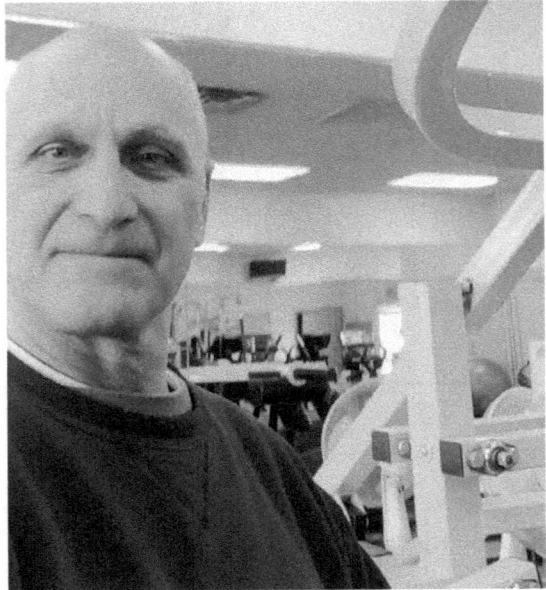

Gym selfie

Selfie with a buddy

Bathroom selfie

Sad selfie

Couple selfie

Groupie, group, or ussie selfie

Duckface selfie

Beach selfie

Family selfie

Vacation selfie

Party selfie

Car selfie

Pouting selfie

Crying (sad) selfie

Sleeping selfie

Pet selfie

7 Picture Play

One of the great things you can do with selfies is play like a kid, an adult, or an artist. There are hundreds of photo editors, filters, special effects, and apps to create strange, fun images. Add ears and a beard; change your face to a lion; play with special effects to create Halloween-like critters. There are no limits on how you can play with your selfie.

Check out some of the following special effects.

Kaleidoscope

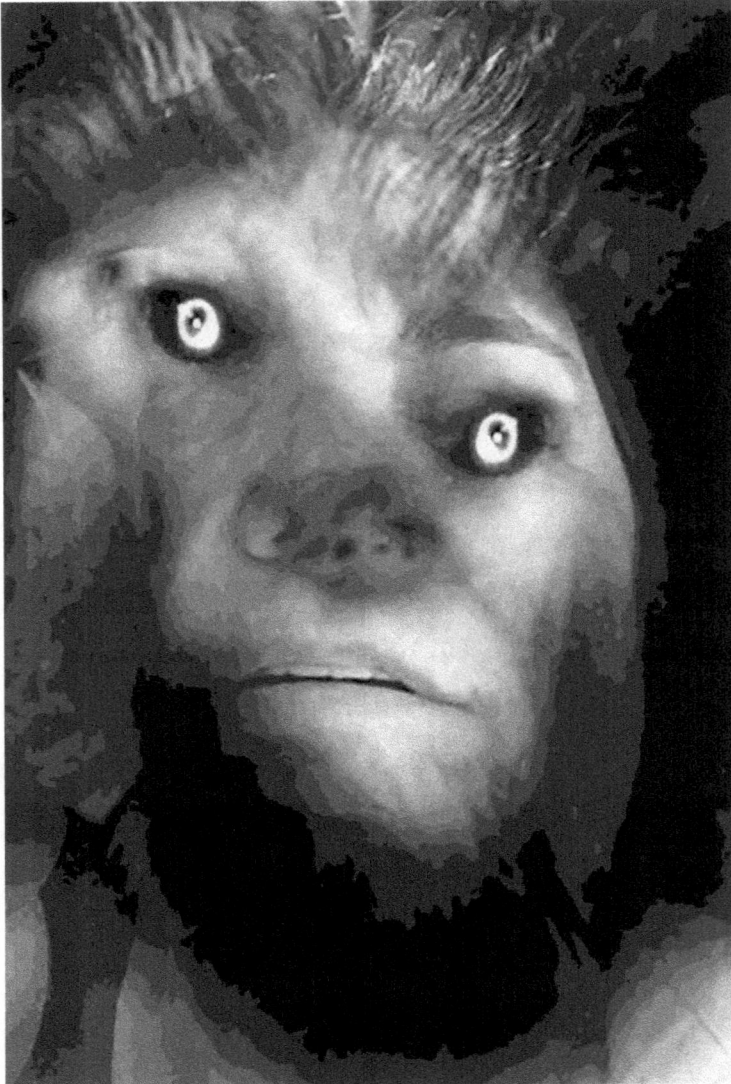

Monster Me

Scary Cartoon

Animal Faces

Alien From Another Galaxy

8 What's Your Message?

Do you know what your selfie *really* says? A picture is worth a thousand words and in a selfie all those words are about you. Read the statements below and circle each one **T** (**true**) or **F** (**false**).

T or F   1. Props can make you look like a showoff.

T or F   2. Cartoons, avatars, and other non-human images are good replacements for your selfie.

T or F   3. "Duck faces" are always appealing.

T or F   4. Adding pets, babies, kids, or others in your selfie profile pictures make it seem like you're hiding from the camera.

T or F   5. Women who make themselves look too sexy and men who look too buff can be a turn-off.

T or F 6. Risky selfies are great.

T or F 7. Sad selfies turn people off.

T or F 8. Extreme close-ups aren't always appealing.

T or F 9. Backgrounds don't count.

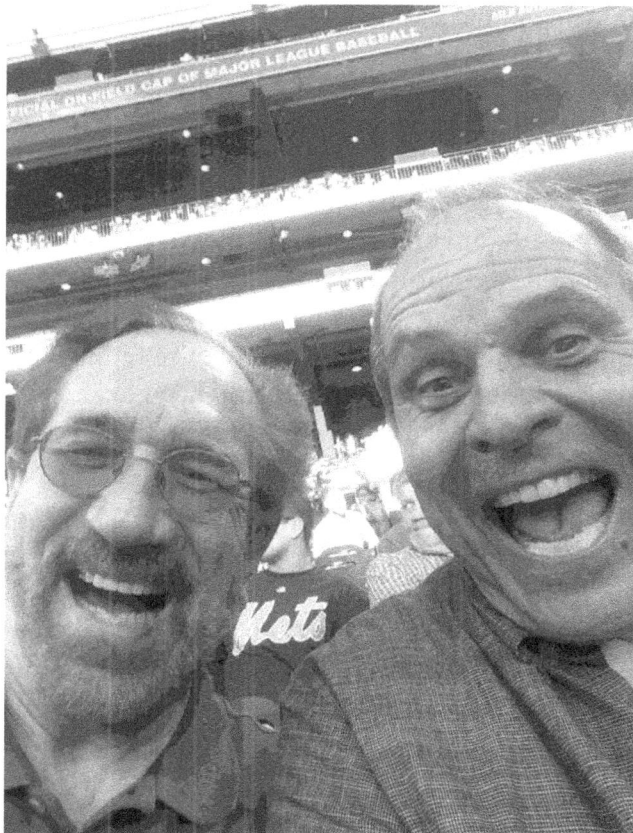

Your message revealed

Read the following to see what your selfie is really saying to the world.

1. True – Props can send the wrong message. If there's too much bling, expensive jewelry, flashy cars, etc. you will look like a showoff.

2. False – Non-human images can make it look like you're shy or avoiding the camera. If the images fit – such as a book cover for an author, a zombie for a makeup artist, or a wild animal for a zoologist, it works.

3. False – The "duck face" or pout where the lips are thrust out or pressed together in a pucker was made popular by celebrities like Kim Kardashian. It may look OK on them but not on you. It screams "look at me" and comes off as silly or annoying. *Buzzfeed* reports that the latest duck face is the "sparrow face" – with wide open eyes and slightly parted mouth that makes you look "like you're a baby bird waiting" for a tasty worm.

4. True – No one is interested in a selfie where you're hiding behind someone or something. The big question is why? Why do you need to keep yourself away from the main picture? Maybe you're shy or have something to hide?

5. True – Too sexy and too buff can turn off people looking for normal connections rather than physical competition.

6. False – Risky selfies can lead to injuries and even death. People do dangerous things like take selfies from a moving vehicle, at the edge of a cliff, with wild animals, weapons, and other hazardous situations. One campaign on how to take safe selfies warns, "A cool selfie could cost you your life."

7. True – People don't want to hang out with someone who is sad, downbeat, or negative. Take selfies where you look happy and appealing. Job applicants who appear happy are usually preferred by employers looking for positive representatives of their company. Employers often check online selfies on sites like Facebook and Linked In.

8. True – Many people think that extreme close-ups are flattering. Think about it. Who wants to see every blemish, line, or mark on your skin? That's why professionals use make-up and photo editing so they look picture perfect.

9. False – Backgrounds always count. A background shouldn't dominate unless it's more important than the picture of you. If your selfie "story" is more about the location, a good background is important. If it's about you or your group only a hint of background is necessary.

9 Tips for Picture Perfect

Everyone wants a great selfie. Create selfies that say "you" and score a lot of likes. Use the following tips to help you take that picture perfect.

*Good eye contact.

*Get comfortable – avoid squinting, grimacing, and harsh shadows.

*Watch out for extreme makeup, clothes, or anything that detracts from you.

*Find a "happy place" that will show up in your photo.

*Look approachable and confident.

*Use the best light – either natural or standing near a window.

*Hold the camera high (above your head) to make it artsy-looking.

*Smile or do something cheerful.

*Be careful using filters.

*Check out the background – is it what you want to say?

*Try editing - most people do. Make sure the result looks natural not fake.

*Have the light in front of you rather than behind or back-lit.

*If you're in bright sun, watch out for shadows that ruin the image.

*Take a lot of shots then pick the one you like best.

*Be yourself.

*Have a good time. It shows!

10 Our Selfie Culture

On top of the Empire State Building people are taking selfies with the view in the background. Wherever you go – Grand Canyon, Hollywood, and Mount Rushmore, selfies define our culture.

A person who wants to date someone from an online site asks for an extra selfie for assurance. A teen posts hourly selfie Facebook updates of a baseball game. A family takes selfies on vacation and texts them to the grandparents.

There are selfies of royalty, politicians snapping their images, even the Pope. Photo bombers slip inside someone else's selfie and thieves break in homes, take what they want, and post selfies of themselves in the act.

Selfies are a celebrated part of our culture. Studies, books, blogs, and videos feature selfies. There are selfie contests, campaigns, branding, and Olympics.

Some people argue that selfies are a type of narcissism; others say they're indicators of mental illness.

In a world where physical appearance means so much, selfies give the illusion that you can define yourself and be in control of your image. They put you on the same page as celebrities – even when *their* selfies may be tasteless and inappropriate. Judgement is often shaky when speed (posting) is more important than thinking it through.

All of which can be very hazardous to a selfie designed to get a lot of likes or, at best, some laughs. Too many dreadful selfies pop up online. How many unflattering ones have you seen?

While selfies began as self-portraits, they evolved to mean something different in today's culture. They continue to progress. New technology, new poses, and selfie videos are all part of our hi-tech culture. We can only guess tomorrow's trends.

It is in unguarded moments that the features are the tell-tales of the mind.

James Lendall Basford, 1845-1915, Watchmaker, Author, Philosopher

11 I Selfie Therefore I Am

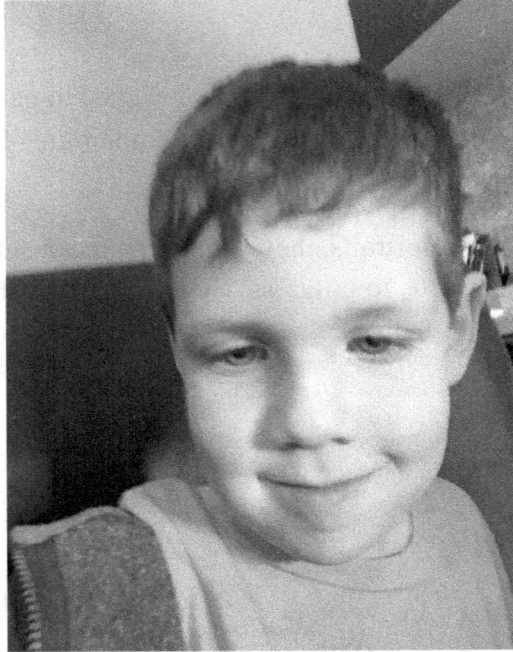

How old do you have to be to selfie?

A selfie is a frozen moment in time – a way to immortalize ourselves and compete with billions of others that share our planet today and billions yet to come. It's a purely democratic way to celebrate ourselves and our worlds - show anger, playfulness, love, hate, beauty - revealing the entire range of emotions and experiences ready for our smartphones, cameras, and posts.

With a world population of 7.5 billion faces, thoughts, ideas, and backgrounds, where is proof that you exist? How do you draw attention in a global neighborhood?

Selfies prove we're alive and aware.

17th century French philosopher and mathematician, René Descartes, believed that most everything can be faked, leading to serious questions about the true nature of life. He decided that thought is the only proof of existence:

I think therefore I am.

Move forward four centuries into technology that spans the planet (and space), complicated ideas that compete every day, and the statement gets updated.

I selfie therefore I am.

Business grabbed the idea – you can purchase *I selfie therefore I am* tote bags, canvases, belt buckles, papers, books . . . the list continues to grow.

Whether you're a child or adult, celebrity or regular person, selfies put you on the map. They're connected to everything from parties, business, and a shout out for attention. It's a documentation of oneself – proof you live and breathe in a crowded digital world. Selfies were born from human fascination with one's own image – just watch what happens when people selfie in a mirror.

12 The Good, the Bad, and the Unexpected!

Selfies bring out the best and worst in us.

There is an odd trend of taking selfies in very inappropriate place like funerals, memorials, and grim monuments. Check out the Tumblr site called "Selfies at Funerals" that includes funeral parlor bathroom shots, grieving shots, silly and smiling mourning images. One caption, "my friend took a selfie at a funeral and I didn't realize his dead grandma was in the background."

That might be cool for a Halloween gag but is it appropriate for real life?

The most infamous funeral selfies were taken at a memorial for South African leader and world hero, Nelson Mandela. Former President Barack Obama, while sitting next to his scowling wife, took a selfie of himself and then Prime Ministers David Cameron (UK) and Helle Thorning-Schmidt (Denmark) during the service. Some dubbed it "the selfie seen 'round the world" – claiming it created an international incident.

It went viral. People love political selfies, along with seasonal "political" statements and critics.

Unfortunately, there's no limit to funny or tasteless selfies that go viral.

Consider the tourist who snapped a selfie as police tried to talk down a suicidal jumper from the Brooklyn Bridge or the doctor who shot selfies of his famous patient, under anesthesia, in surgery.

Then there are those selfies – the ones we love to see, that take us off the planet and into the unexpected, like the following shot taken by Milan Nykodym as he patrolled Icelandic airspace.

Creative Commons

Some of my favorite selfies were taken from space!

NASA [Public domain], via Wikimedia Commons

Astronauts Samantha Cristoforetti and Terry Virts joined the trend with their selfie from the Tranquility Module in the International Space Station. While you can't take a selfie on Mars or Venus yet, there are props that can make it look like you're there!

13 Naked Selfies

andyspb (http://creativecommons.org/licenses/by/2.0)
via Wikimedia Commons

Are you one of the 70% of people online who received or sent a naked selfie or sexting message?

Hackers (and others) love to spread nude and lewd naked selfies all over social media. From celebrities to amateurs, and politicians to everyday people, naked selfies and sexting are increasingly popular. There are websites, tweeters, girls, teens, moms, and dads involved. It's not hard to hack into the cloud where naked selfies are stored and grabbed illegally.

Why would people want their naked selfies in the cloud – waiting to be used or misused – by anyone who can do whatever they want?

Celebrities like Jennifer Lawrence, Miley Cyrus, and Kanye West all posted naked or seductive selfies. Royals like Prince Harry (before Meghan Markle) also participated. Nude Geraldo Rivera, trying to show he has the best body of any 70 year old, posted online (who really wants to see?). It doesn't stop there. Justin Bieber, Ryan Gosling, Zac Efron . . . there are actors, actresses, celebrities, models . . . the list is endless. Even teachers, principals, and students are doing it. If a child is underage it might mean trouble for the participating adult.

Naked selfies are self-posted, too-often hacked, sent through online exchanges, and spread around the internet. There are also naked selfies posted in revenge, from an ex or spurned someone, looking to make trouble. Caveat emptor – let the buyer beware!

Anthony Weiner, An Infamous Sexter

Weiner is a former New York congressman, and mayoral candidate. He was married to Hillary Clinton's chief aide, Huma Abedin. He lost his career and marriage because of uncontrolled, obsessive sexting.

It began as a "mistake" – Weiner posted photos of his crotch on social media instead of sending them privately to a 21-year old female college student. The error was removed but not fast enough. People took screen shots. It went viral. Congressman Weiner initially denied sending the photo, claiming it wasn't him. It was too late. Earlier images surfaced. He eventually admitted to "messages and photos of an explicit nature with about six women over the last three years," adding that he never "met or had a physical relationship with any of them."

Two days later *Breitbart* posted more photos and it went viral. Politicians from both parties protested, forcing Weiner to resign on June 16, 2011.

Weiner, a popular politician, resurfaced in 2013 as a candidate for New York City mayor. He held a comfortable lead in the primary until new sexting photos appeared. Weiner confessed. He begged the public for forgiveness. They didn't buy it. He plummeted in the polls, along with a public demand to quit the race. He vowed to fight. It didn't work. Bill de Blasio won the Democratic primary and Mayoral race in a landslide.

Once again, in 2016, *The New York Post* reported that Weiner was back to sexting, showing him lying in bed with his toddler son sleeping next to him. Weiner was sexting with an underage girl. His wife left him and a year later, and Weiner was sentenced to 21 months in prison.

14 Selfie Studies

Selfies is a popular subject for research in psychology and social psychology. The following are some interesting findings.

*Men who think "highly of themselves" tend to post more selfies.

*Women aged 16-25 take the most selfies.

*One in five adults of all ages have experienced sexting.

*Women who base their self-worth on how they look share more photos online and have larger networks on social media.

*One in five people take selfies while driving a car. Males ages 25-35 are most likely to take driving selfies.

*One study found that there are three types of selfie takers: communicators, self-publicists, and autobiographers. Where do you fit?

*People love taking selfies but don't like seeing selfies of others. It's called the selfie paradox.

*People who take many selfies tend to think they're more attractive and likeable.

*Men who posted more than the average number of selfies scored higher in narcissism and psychopathy.

*In one study, when students saw more sexual photos of their peers they assumed they were having unprotected sex and sex with strangers and decided it was okay.

*People who post a lot of selfies can alienate friends, family, and colleagues.

*Selfitis is defined by The American Psychiatric Association as the inflation of the ego by taking too many selfies. They identified it as a mental disorder.

*More than 44% of 18-24 year olds and 34% of 25-34 year olds have used their cellphones to receive sexts.

15 Selfie Psychology

Your selfie might be saying more than you want. Professionals, expert researchers, and social psychologists have conducted numerous studies to see if selfies correlate with social, psychological, and emotional health.

Temperament is often revealed in selfies and selfie behavior. Check out some of the following traits that can be exposed.

Temperament	Selfie
Agreeable	Gives a positive feeling, tends to hold the camera lower
Conscientious	Hides the location of selfie perhaps because of privacy concerns
Emotionally unstable	Duckface, pouting, tight-lipped
Poor self-image	A selfie that cries "Look at me!"
Poor relationships	Excessive selfies that replace experiencing real life
Need to show off	Solo selfies
Extrovert	Posts a lot of selfies
High self-esteem in men	Excessive posting
Need to feel or appear included	Group selfies
Narcissism in women	Posting frequent status updates, selfies, and links
Poor self-esteem	Selfitis, selfie Syndrome, Selfie Addiction, obsessive posting
Optimism	Selfies that affirm and empower

Dangerous Selfies

Too often, selfies are connected to danger, risky behavior, and even violence.

Risky selfies have led to injury or death. Taking a selfie from the top of a moving train, falling off a cliff, or fatally shooting yourself while posing with loaded guns have all contributed to selfie danger, risky behavior, and violence.

Perhaps the most gruesome are the domestic violence selfies – before and after shots of bloody beatings and assaults.

There are outrageous stories like the India teenager who drowned because his friends were too busy taking selfies to rescue him or the 19-year old who tried to kill himself because he couldn't get the perfect selfie.

"I lost my friends, my education, my health, and almost my life," he cried.

With so many selfies it's no surprise that there's a very dark side which leads to danger, risky behavior, violence, and injury or death

Selfie behavior and emotional problems

Body dysmorphic disorder is when people constantly think about real or imagined shortcomings in how they look. It's not always obvious to others. The person might take and post many selfies, trying to get rid of "flaws" but never quite succeeding.

Narcissism is healthy, but in some cases, unhealthy. The healthy type is being able to appreciate yourself and your accomplishments. The unhealthy type is feeling more important than others, claiming to be superior, believing that you're better than everyone, and having a need for others to worship you. Unhealthy narcissism can come out in selfie behavior. Men who posted more photos of themselves tend to be narcissistic when they repeatedly show off with selfies.

Negative self-image is when people set impossible standards for success, popularity, or how they appear to the world, but really see themselves as inferior. They are often perfectionists and high achievers who never reach their impossible goals. Selfies are a way to be seen as perfect. Ironically, obsessive posting of selfies increases comparisons and can make negative self-image worse.

Obsessive Compulsive Disorder (OCD) is common, chronic, and long-lasting. It consists of *obsessions* or repeated anxious thoughts and *compulsions* or repetitive behaviors in response to obsessive thoughts. The APA (American Psychiatric Association) defined "*Selfitis*" as an obsessive compulsive disorder where people constantly take and post selfies.

Psychopathic Traits are more common with men who post a lot of selfies online. Psychopathic traits fall on a scale; someone can have a few or many. These traits include no conscience, no empathy, selfishness, grandiosity, risk-taking, and the inability to love. Several studies have found that psychopathic traits are linked to obsessively taking and posting selfies.

Selfie Addiction

Addicts can't stop. Whether it's drugs, gambling, or selfies, addiction means being psychologically, physically, or obsessively bound to a substance, thing, or activity. Someone who can't stop taking selfies and obsessively posting them is often called a selfie addict. Research has found that selfie addicts tend to be extroverts and social exhibitionists.

Other studies suggest that they may suffer from low self-esteem. People like Anthony Weiner, a selfie/sexting addict, has a mental illness similar to a heroin addict who can't give up drugs.

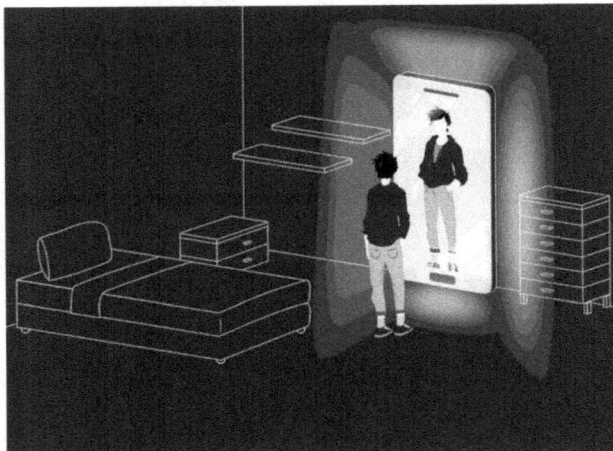

16 The Selfie Economy

Morph your selfie into a zombie. Go bug-eyed or thermal.

There are hundreds of apps that will transform a selfie into almost anything. Plunk your selfie on a milk carton, travel to Mars, appear on TV, or put a tiger on your head in the middle of New York City.

It's cheap and easy in the selfie economy.

Selfies are newbies in the global economy although the word has been around since the first selfie hashtag in 2004. The idea really caught on when *Apple* introduced a front-facing camera to the iPhone. Three years later in 2013, "selfie" was declared the "word of the year" by Oxford English Dictionaries. The following year Ellen DeGeneres took a selfie with a group of movie stars at the Academy Awards. There were 3 million retweets. They used a *Galaxy Note 3* – a Samsung phone and the $20 million sponsor of the show.

DeGeneres' selfie was valued at up $1 billion because of its worldwide sharing on social media – and that's before the Samsung product placement. Here's the irony. Whether it's *Samsung* or your picnic at the beach, it works the same way. President Obama, Pope Francis, and hundreds of other high profile faces reside alongside of you.

That means business. Big business.

Selfie accessories have blasted the marketplace. Ira Kalb, President of Kalb & Associates, and Associate Professor of Business at USC, writes "Selfies have now caught the fancy of the business world; they are effectively used to promote products, services, brands, [and] e-commerce."

There are selfie sticks, hairbrushes, tripods, remotes, timers, apps, lights, even a selfie booth for your party. You can find selfie props of all sizes and shapes, t-shirts, books, holders, backlights . . . the list is endless. In 2014, *Time* listed the selfie stick as one of the best inventions of the year. Within a year, hundreds of thousands were sold around the world, forcing bans at venues like museums and music festivals. It's a product that's everywhere now.

Special flashes and 360-degree digital cameras placed in the center of a round table are readily available.

The selfie economy boasts more than just hardware. Consider three popular business uses:

1. Marketing that guides, engages, and promotes customer purchases.
2. Advertising and publicity.
3. Selfie campaigns that build non-celebrity brand ambassadors.

That's the short list. Make-up, clothing, hair color, product placement all make your business look good. There are stores with internet-connected dressing rooms. Others use virtual mirrors to scan faces and superimpose new looks. Brand placements on non-celebrity selfies are becoming a powerful asset in marketing.

Get the picture?

17 The Future is Now

The surge in selfies and accessories is growing. Selfies are not going away – they're spreading to different venues like video and drones. Augmented reality create opportunities to produce selfies that put people anywhere, anytime, anyplace. Can you imagine a selfie of you, dancing on Mars or Jupiter?

Some people believe that the selfie culture breeds unhealthy narcissism, encouraging more obsessions with social media. They argue that eventually people will return to the "old" normal.

Don't count on it. Selfies have made us *more* intimate with technology. The need to connect has been expanded and redefined – without requiring physical contact or being in the same place. According to new research reported by *Xperia,* people are more open than ever before to "embrace" selfies in many different venues.

A recent survey of 6500 people identified 9 ways where selfies will become part of daily life in the coming years.

1. Dating
2. Medical
3. Banking
4. Leisure
5. Gym/workouts
6. Measuring clothes
7. Retail
8. Social currency
9. Robots

Who knows what children, born into a culture of selfies, will imagine and invent when they grow up?

18 Fascinating Facts, Memes, and Stats

Everyone loves them – tiny bits of news, info, or behavior. People love to share them! Here are a few you'll want to spread around.

*In November, 2013, the word "selfie" was declared "word of the year" by the Oxford English Dictionary.

*In February, 2016 a U.S. Federal judge ruled that a monkey cannot own the copyright to his selfies.

*One of the most famous celebrity selfies was taken during the 86th Academy Awards when Ellen DeGeneres took a group selfie of Oscar Celebrities. Within 24 hours it had been retweeted almost 3 million times.

*According to a report from the *International Business Times,* millennials will take more than 25,000 selfies during their lifetime.

*Selfies can be dangerous. People take them while driving, setting up hazardous situations like walking train tracks, and posing with wild animals. High-risk selfie takers can be wounded or killed when posing with handguns that fire accidentally, falling from cliffs, or drowning.

*Nearly half of selfie-related deaths were in India; 75% were male; and most among 21-year olds.

*Generally, women take more selfies than men until they reach age 40. Then it reverses and over 40 men take more selfies than women.

*The first known selfie-related death was March 15, 2014 when a man electrocuted himself on top of a train while taking a selfie.

*More than one million selfies are taken around the world each day.

*The countries with the most selfies are Australia, USA, and Canada in that order.

*Some people become selfie-obsessed or selfie-addicts.

*People who take a lot of gym and workout selfies might have body image problems.

*Most people edit their selfies - roughly 70% of women and 50% of men do it while only 36% admit it.

*Selfies are 30% of the photos taken by people 18-24.

*In 2014 the word selfie was officially accepted in the game *Scrabble*.

*A 2015 study found that 20% of young people from the UK took selfies while driving a car.

*The *Urban Dictionary* describes a selfie as "the beginning of the end of intelligent civilization."

*Selfie apps and accessories have become a big business.

*Selfie sticks have been banned in various places including museums, concert festivals, and amusement parks.

*Scientists can't decide whether selfies *hurt* or *help* self-esteem.

*A photo bomber is someone who pops into a selfie (or other photograph) uninvited – sometimes it's on purpose, sometimes it's a joke, and often it happens in very embarrassing ways.

*In 1966, Buzz Aldrin took the first selfie in space.

*Most are upbeat (80% positive, 20% negative).

*Selfies are destined to appear throughout social media such as Facebook, Twitter, Instagram, Snapchat, and other popular sites.

*A selfie can define you – be careful.

*There are trends in selfies like groupies, foot selfies, shameless selfies, naked selfies, gym selfies, sex selfies, travel selfies . . . anything goes.

*Video selfies are very popular.

*Selfies are for all ages - young, old, and in-between.

*Selfies can be for lovers.

19 What Makes a Good Selfie?

Most people take selfies without much thinking. What do you really want your selfie to say? The following are different aspects of a selfie. Consider them. What's important to you? How do you tell the world who you really are? What message do you want to put out there?

Don't forget where you are, who you're with, and the story behind it!

Read the list carefully. Circle what's most appealing to *you*.

Selfie Aspect	My picture perfect
Facial expression	Sad, frowning
	Seductive, sexy
	Happy, smiling
	Sneering, nasty
	Welcoming
	Angry, mean, scary
	Silly
	Blank
Eyes	Closed
	Open
	Squinting
	Suspicious, wary, questioning
	Happy, laughing, friendly
	Sad
	Sexy
Mouth	Smiling, laughing, friendly
	Frowning
	Pouting, duck-faced
	Clenched, tight lips
	Open, hungry
	No expression

Selfie Aspect	My picture perfect
Hair	Windblown, wild
	Sexy
	Natural
	Covering my eyes
	Highly styled
	Traditional
Body Pose	Relaxed, peaceful
	Tense, suspicious
	Gentle, nurturing
	Aggressive, fighting
	Natural, comfortable
	Sexy
	Uncomfortable
	Awkward
Background	None
	Busy, active
	Scary, dark, risky
	Nature
	Bright, lively, fun
	Travel site
	Pleasant, feel-good
	Other people

Using the words you circled, list the details that make your picture perfect selfie.

Selfie Aspect	My picture perfect selfie
Facial expression	
Eyes	
Mouth	
Hair	
Body Pose	
Background	

Now go out and have fun!

Take picture perfect selfies!

Read cutting-edge Book Web Minis

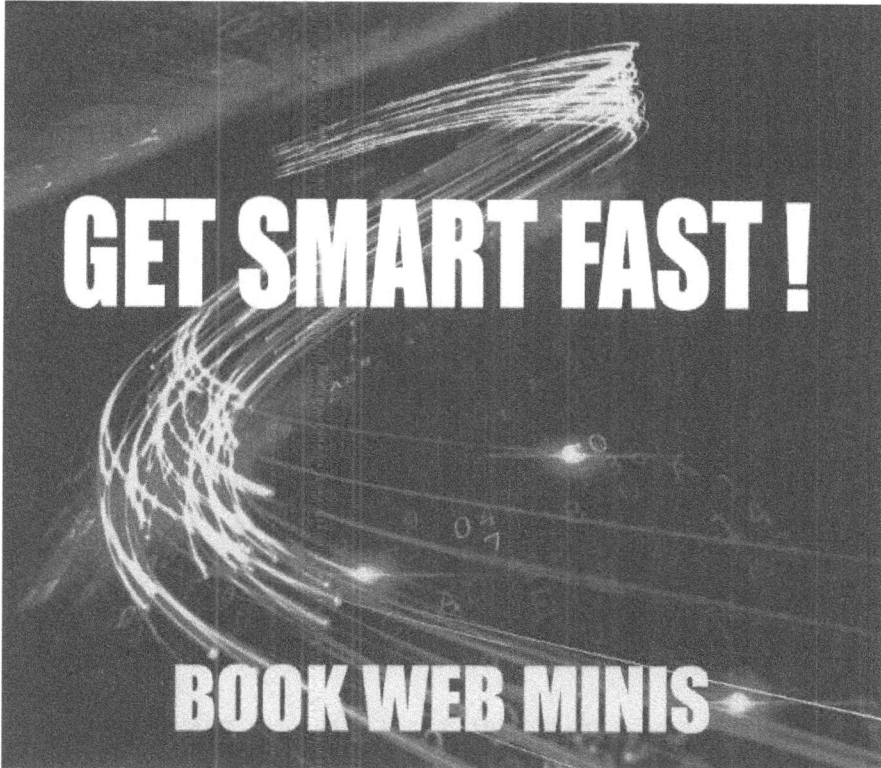
Book Web Minis are fun, fast, and hot. Mini books (50-70 pages long) explore up-to-the-minute facts, photos, content, and quizzes to make you the pro. Share with friends, family, and colleagues. Don't wait – get them from Amazon.com

Bestselling Titles:
Paranormal Is My Normal
SOARING
Timepieces: Yesterday's Stories Today
PocketCash: Your Way
Photo Power: Hidden Stories

www.bookwebminis.com

Check out Book Web Fiction

Amazon #1 Bestsellers!

Page turners bursting with haunted family trees, strange lovers, chilling photo insights, and twisted psychopaths burst into life. *Broken Books* reinvent the thriller – blending fact, fiction, and photos into riveting stories you'll never forget. Go to amazon.com to purchase these bestsellers in eBook, print (black & white), and collector's edition (full color print).

Contemporary thrillers:

Broken By Truth (Book 1)

Broken By Birth (Book 2)

Broken By Evil (Book 3)

Don't miss Book Web Historical Fiction

Go back in time to discover how good and evil thrived in the past. Meet the ancestors of the characters in the first three *Broken Books* and follow their legacy.

*Broken By Madness (*Book 4, Dutch New Amsterdam, 1654)

Broken By Men (Book 5, Spain and Portugal, 1490s)

Broken By Kings (Book 6, Sao Tome, Africa, 1494)

Broken: The Prequel (Book 7, Spanish Inquisition, 15th century)

www.hauntedfamilytrees.com

Links

Dr. Jeri Fink: jeri@jerifink.com

Donna Paltrowitz: donnapaltrowitz@gmail.com

Bookweb Minis: www.bookwebminis.com

Bookweb Fiction: www.hauntedfamilytrees.com

Photo Insights (original "feel-good" photos delivered weekly, for free, into you email box):

http://hauntedfamilytrees.com/landing-page

MY NOTES

www.ingramcontent.com/pod-product-compliance
Lightning Source LLC
Chambersburg PA
CBHW081721270326
41933CB00017B/3249